purposed to impact

Discover and Activate Your Higher Calling

by Kendall Nelson

table of contents

First let me say how excited I am that you've chosen to take this journey. It takes a lot to stop and ask ourselves, *What is it God really wants me to do with my life?* It takes even more to set out on a mission to find it. It takes humility. It takes intentionality. It takes a true desire to know God and know who He created you to be... and why. *Purposed to Impact* will get you there.

A little backstory...

It took several revisions of my personal game plan—and countless hours in prayer—for me to finally grasp where I felt God was leading me all along. The concept for this book was birthed out of my own self-discovery process.

Always the girl with the plan, I've known since I was a little girl what I wanted to be when I grew up: the first girl in the NBA and a corporate lawyer in the off-season. And no one could tell me otherwise! By high school though, I'd become disenchanted with playing the game, and I suffered a knee injury to boot. Thus the vision was refined: I'd become a sports agent instead. I studied business in college, still planning to go to law school thereafter and build a client base of pro football and basketball players for whom I'd negotiate playing contracts and endorsement deals. But the summer after my sophomore year of undergrad, the unthinkable happened.

A devastating accident shattered my world, shook my faith, and shredded my plans. We lost Stephanie, my best friend and the most loving, genuine, and faith-driven person I've ever known. She was 21, and no one saw it coming. But God never ends the story in tragedy; something beautiful always comes from even the most crushing experiences—if you choose to see it. Several of Stephanie's friends gave their lives to Christ as a result of her impact on them, and her legacy of love continues to imprint the hearts of so many others—from her family and friends to the perfect strangers she'd stop, sit and talk with any and everywhere she went.

Realizing Stephanie's beautiful, abundant and impactful legacy made me consider my own. In only 21 years, she'd managed to affect literally hundreds of people just by the way she cared for them in her everyday interactions—the 212-car funeral procession proved it. *What did I have to show for my life?* I wondered. A decent GPA and some pretty superficial aspirations were all I could come up with. I knew that had to change. I wanted to honor Stephanie's legacy by living out my own, striving to make a positive difference in a way that truly mattered.

Thus, the vision was refined further, and it has continued to take shape over the last several years. With God's help, I realized I could use my love for strategy and planning to help people and organizations use their gifts to serve others in a meaningful and measureable way. And with God never overlooking a single detail, He's tied it all together and allowed me opportunities to work with all kinds of sports organizations across the world—my ultimate dream. What can I say? He is faithful!

Through it all, my faith has been my anchor and the single source of clarity that has helped me to recognize how to put my gifts and talents to their best, most valuable use. It's that same clarity I want to help you find. That's what *Purposed to Impact* is all about.

What you can expect...

Purposed to Impact is an exciting and empowering adventure of Bible-led self-discovery that's as practical as it is scriptural. With reflection prompts, worksheets and step-by-step planning activities, this book is designed to guide you through the process of identifying your skills, gifts, and passions and leveraging them to build and live (not just leave) a legacy of love and impact.

As believers, all of us share two inherent directives: 1) to love God with all of our heart, soul, mind, and strength, and 2) to love our neighbor as we love ourselves (see Mark 12:30–31). These are the greatest commandments, and they are what defines the impact we each were created to generate. By actively embracing God's supernatural influence and accepting His mission and purpose for us as Christians, we will live a life in which His love for us, our love for Him, and our love for each other abound. In doing so, we reflect Him—His nature, His character, His compassion—to those in our spheres of influence and generate eternal value.

By finding creative ways to use what you've been given to reflect God's love to others, you'll devise an action plan through four key stages that will guide you to living out your higher calling: Discover, Dream, Define, Do. As you come to a better understanding of what God has called you to do, you will be able to apply these principles to your own life by understanding how, with God's help, you can fearlessly launch into your purpose.

Each leg of this journey equips you with Biblical principles upon which to build your faith so that you can start to see the purpose for your life as God designed it. As you work through this devotional, you allow God to reveal Himself, and His plans, to you. You'll find practical tips and action steps at the end of each section to propel you through this purpose discovery and activation process. Take as much time as you need to complete each action item before moving on to the next. Be thoughtful. Be intentional. Be prayerful in seeking God's direction and in discerning the path He's leading you on.

Whether it be for a business endeavor, ministry involvement, community service work or personal growth, the *Purposed to Impact* experience will equip and empower you to live out your God-given purpose and positively impact your world.

I encourage you to really dive into this experience and allow God to open your mind and heart to His great plans for your life. If you'll trust Him and be faithful to the process, you'll find yourself living a purpose-full life that generates eternal value not only for you but also for those around you.

Ephesians 2:10 says, *"For we are God's masterpiece. He has created us anew in Christ Jesus, so we can do the good things he planned for us long ago." (NLT)* God has very intentionally instilled in you passions, gifts and dreams that He wants to use for a very special purpose. They are His investment in you, and it's up to you to determine what kind of return He will get. Use the tools in this book to find where and how they all fit together, and start living on purpose, with purpose.

discover
your mission and purpose

Lord Jesus, please open my heart to a realization of what You've called me to do as a believer in Your Truth. Thank You for creating me with a unique mission and purpose to serve You and advance Your Kingdom. Help me to understand and pursue them wholeheartedly.

your God-given mission

And all of this is a gift from God, who brought us back to himself through Christ. And God has given us this task of reconciling people to him. (2 Corinthians 5:18, NLT)

Webster defines mission as "a specific task with which a person or a group is charged". God created each one of us with a specific mission in mind and a preconceived idea of who we could become and what we could accomplish for His Kingdom.

As Christians, we all share a single, collective mission: to live a life pleasing to and representative of Christ. Upon creation, mankind was made in the image of God—His perfect reflection. God's intention was for us to be His living, breathing representatives and carry out our daily responsibilities as He saw fit. But as we learned from Adam and Eve in the Garden of Eden, we have a choice in the matter. The experiences we have, the choices we make, and the people we're surrounded with have a profound impact on our lives and our ability to achieve our God-given mission.

So how do we please and represent Christ? The way we carry ourselves, the things we talk about and involve ourselves in, the company we keep, and the places we go all reflect a lifestyle of our choosing. In order to actively engage in our God-given mission, we must intentionally endeavor to align those things with the values and priorities embodied by Jesus Christ.

CONSIDER THIS:
What did Jesus' earthly ministry reveal about His values and priorities? How does your current lifestyle align with those priorities?

TAKE ACTION:
On the next page, consider the godly characteristics you'd like to reflect and those that others currently see in you. Brainstorm some ways you can embrace your God-given mission and more actively and accurately reflect Christ in your everyday life.

what am I reflecting?

Characteristics I'd like to reflect:

Characteristics others say I reflect:

Things to keep doing:
For things on both lists above, what is it I'm already doing to help others see this trait in me?

Things to start doing (or do more often):
What actions can I take to better reflect the characteristics I'd like others to see in me?

notes

notes

"For you will certainly carry out God's purpose, however you act, but it makes a difference to you whether you serve like Judas or like John." – C. S. Lewis

free space

"God's definition of what matters is pretty straightforward. He measures our lives by how we love." – Francis Chan

free space

"The fact that you are still alive assures you that God has something for you to accomplish." – Rodney A. Winters

your God-given purpose

Yes, you will be enriched in every way so that you can always be generous. And when we take your gifts to those who need them, they will thank God. (2 Corinthians 9:11, NLT)

If *mission* is our what, *purpose* is our why. God takes joy in blessing us, but He does so with very specific intentions. We are blessed in order to pass along those blessings to others. When we do this, we reflect the true nature of Christ, causing those whom we bless to give thanks to God and be drawn back toward Him. That's the purpose behind our God-given mission.

You are blessed, and it's for a reason! God has deliberately instilled in us specific gifts, has entrusted us with certain resources, and has placed us in intentionally crafted spheres of influence to make an impact on those around us in the way they need to be reached. The challenge for us is keeping others in mind instead of getting caught up in managing our own lives.

The busyness of life and the weight of our responsibilities can make it far too easy to forget our mission to reflect Christ and lead others to Him. We must remember that everything we've been given is to serve this purpose, and there are countless ways we can use what we have to achieve this end.

CONSIDER THIS:
Sometimes the things we take for granted—our financial security, vehicles, homes, etc.—are the very things we can use to make a difference in the lives of others. What are some things you've been blessed with that you could use to serve, bless or empower others?

TAKE ACTION:
Think of someone you can be a blessing to this week. It's important that you see how something you're skilled in can be used to enrich the lives of others and give glory to God.

notes

"I wish to do something Great and Wonderful, but I must start by doing the little things like they were Great and Wonderful." – Albert Einstein

notes

"When I let go of what I am, I become what I might be." – Lao Tzu

free space

*"Why you? Because there is no one better. Why now?
Because tomorrow isn't soon enough." – Donna Brazile*

free space

"The most difficult thing is the decision to act, the rest is merely tenacity."
– Amelia Earhart

your personal mission

God has given each of us the ability to do certain things well. So if God has given you the ability to prophesy, then prophesy whenever you can—as often as your faith is strong enough to receive a message from God. If your gift is that of serving others, serve them well. If you are a teacher, do a good job of teaching. If you are a preacher, see to it that your sermons are strong and helpful. If God has given you money, be generous in helping others with it. If God has given you administrative ability and put you in charge of the work of others, take the responsibility seriously. Those who offer comfort to the sorrowing should do so with Christian cheer. (Romans 12:6–8, TLB)

Each and every one of us was created a unique individual. God did that for a reason! Like all the different parts of the body, we all look and function differently and are strategically located to serve a specific purpose. When we each do our part, the body operates cohesively and is able to achieve its full potential. As believers God called, chose, and fit us together in the same way— each with unique gifts, passions, experiences and a customized part to play. No wonder we're called the body of Christ!

Our mission as believers is to draw others to Christ by reflecting His image and using our gifts to serve in love. We make that personal by figuring out how best we can activate the talents and skills with which we were gifted to make a difference in the lives of others and ultimately reveal Christ through our actions. Whether it's getting involved in ministry at your church, starting or joining a community outreach initiative to help people in need, or using your personal or professional skills to help your church or another organization serve its mission, there are many ways to invest the talents God has given you back into His Kingdom and lead others to Him in doing so.

CONSIDER THIS:

What are your gifts? If you're not sure yet, be diligent in asking God to show you what they are and how you can use them to serve others.

TAKE ACTION:

On the next page, identify your personal mission, which will help answer the "What am I supposed to be doing?" question. Your personal mission lies at the intersection of your gifts and talents, interests and passions, and others' perception of your strengths.

my personal mission

Things I'm good at:

Things I'm passionate about:

MISSION

Things I enjoy doing:

Things others see my strength in:

How can I activate these things with synergy?

notes

"We must believe that we are gifted for something, and that this thing, at whatever cost, must be attained." – Marie Curie

notes

"When we give cheerfully and accept gratefully, everyone is blessed."
– Maya Angelou

free space

"We should certainly count our blessings, but we should also make our blessings count." – Neal A. Maxwell

free space

respond to God's call

The Lord had said to Abram, "Leave your native country, your relatives, and your father's family, and go to the land that I will show you. I will make you into a great nation. I will bless you and make you famous, and you will be a blessing to others. I will bless those who bless you and curse those who treat you with contempt. All the families on earth will be blessed through you." (Genesis 12:1-3, NLT)

When God called Abram, He promised him an abundance of blessings: he would be the father of a great nation, and his name would be known around the world. He would be richly blessed in order to be a blessing to others. But the road ahead would be a challenging one that would lead deep into unfamiliar territory.

Similarly, when God calls each of us to participate in our created purpose, His instructions aren't always the most specific. We might get the "what" or the "where," or even a glimpse of how everything will look when it all comes together, but rarely (if at all) does God's calling come with a step-by-step, fully mapped out and time-stamped guide to achieving our life's mission.

God needed Abram to step out of the comfort zone of his home country and his family if he was to effectively accomplish the mission and purpose set before him. Like Abram, we'll have to trust God's plan for our lives and venture into the unknown if we're going to accomplish what He created us to do. We'll undoubtedly have to leave some people, places and things behind in order to fully embrace our God-given mission and purpose. We can rest assured, however, that God will show us the way and protect us along our journey to living the life He calls us to live.

CONSIDER THIS:
Do you feel like God is leading you in a specific direction? Is there something you feel like you're supposed to do or meant to be?

TAKE ACTION:
On the next page, map out what you believe God's call for your life is. Jot down some of the things you'll have to overcome and some things you'll need to activate in order to answer that call.

heart search

I feel called to...

To accomplish this, I must...

Overcome: ✕ **Activate:**

Obstacle to take down first:

What's the #1 thing I want to overcome?

Step 1: Activate my gifts
Which of my talents will help me start pursuing my calling?

Step 2: Access resources
What additional support might I need along the way?

Step 3: Add faith
What do I need to believe God for?

notes

---

notes

"Never surrender your hopes and dreams to the fateful limitations others have placed on their own lives." – Anthon St. Maarten

free space

"Keep away from people who belittle your ambitions... the really great make you feel that you, too, can become great." – Mark Twain

free space

 "As long as I am breathing, in my eyes, I am just beginning." – Criss Jami

choose to re-engage

Now I will rescue you and make you both a symbol and a source of blessing. So don't be afraid. Be strong, and get on with rebuilding the Temple! (Zechariah 8:13b, NLT)

With the introduction of sin into the world, our direct connection with God was severed, and our ability to reflect Him effortlessly was usurped. Everyday we are bombarded with a myriad of different "images" we can choose to reflect, making it all the more challenging to portray the image of Christ instead of images of beauty, success, individualism, and popularity that our society pushes on us relentlessly.

Even when we find ourselves overrun by worldly influence, there's still hope for us to re-engage in God's mission and purpose for our lives. After Jerusalem fell captive to the Babylonians, God spoke through the prophet Zechariah to encourage the children of Israel to continue rebuilding the temple. They were given the opportunity to start over, and God promises the same for us.

God is faithful to help us get back on track when we've been derailed. In fact, He promises to bless us in spite of our shortcomings! We need only to ask for His help and begin again to pursue the mission and purpose He set for us.

CONSIDER THIS:

What things have derailed you from pursuing your relationship with God and His mission and purpose for your life? Is there anything that is currently standing in the way of you re-engaging with God's mission?

TAKE ACTION:

Everyday we're bombarded by voices and influences that either help or hinder us from truly reflecting God's image and pointing people to Him. On the next page, identify the voices you need to silence and those you need to amplify as you strive to listen for and follow God's voice of truth in your everyday life.

Commit to at least one change that you can implement each day in order to get back on track with achieving God's purpose for your life.

listening for the voice of truth

Voices to silence:

Voices to amplify:

notes

"You must find something that you deeply love and are passionate about and are willing to sacrifice a lot to achieve." – Howard Schultz

notes

free space

"Your beliefs don't make you a better person. Your behavior does."
– Dr. Sukhraj S. Dhillon

free space

"The purpose of life is to contribute in some way to making things better."
– Robert F. Kennedy

your moral imperative

These are the memoirs of Nehemiah son of Hacaliah. In late autumn, in the month of Kislev, in the twentieth year of King Artaxerxes' reign, I was at the fortress of Susa. Hanani, one of my brothers, came to visit me with some other men who had just arrived from Judah. I asked them about the Jews who had returned there from captivity and about how things were going in Jerusalem. They said to me, "Things are not going well for those who returned to the province of Judah. They are in great trouble and disgrace. The wall of Jerusalem has been torn down, and the gates have been destroyed by fire." When I heard this, I sat down and wept. In fact, for days I mourned, fasted, and prayed to the God of heaven. (Nehemiah 1:1–4, NLT)

What's the one thing that immediately gets under your skin or tugs at your heartstrings when you're listening to the news or reading about what's going on in the world? Those things that really affect you—issues like injustice, poverty, or inequality—can point to the hidden passion fueling your moral imperative.

When Nehemiah heard about Jerusalem's destroyed city wall and the distraught state of his people back home, he was immediately moved to tears. In that moment, he discovered his moral imperative—an unshakeable desire to help restore his people and his homeland—and was compelled to do something about it.

Like Nehemiah, each of us has something we are passionate about that drives us to action. It's that thing you just can't ignore, that you just *have* to do something about until a wrong has been made right. And maybe there's more than one! It could be fighting for a cure to a disease that has impacted a friend or family member; feeding the hungry; caring for the elderly, the sick, or shut-in; educating our next generation of leaders... the possibilities are endless. And maybe, like Nehemiah, it will take someone opening your eyes to a cause you don't yet know about or fully understand to find something that really resonates with you. That's ok! Life is a journey, and through our daily experiences, we are constantly gaining knowledge and, as a result, the ability to improve our current realities.

One thing is for certain: God wants each of us to find ways to apply our gifts and passions to serve others just as He did (and still does!).

CONSIDER THIS:
Has God placed a specific burden on your heart—something you're passionate about working on or helping with? If you're not sure yet, ask Him!

TAKE ACTION:
A moral imperative is a strongly felt principle that compels you to take action in a given situation. It is a closely held belief, triggered by your conscience that, for believers in Christ and His Truth, can manifest as God's divine voice speaking through your human spirit. Identifying your Personal Moral Imperative will help you discover meaningful ways that you can make a difference.

Think about how you can work to correct a personally important problem facing your community or the world at large using what you've been given. Take time to map out your Personal Moral Imperative using the diagram on the next page.

Be prayerful in this process, as the Personal Moral Imperative you identify will serve as a guide for the rest of this journey. Spend time in prayer with a focused intention to hear God's voice as you look to discern your passions and moral identity. If your heart and mind are open, God will impress something upon your heart and point you in the right direction during your meditation time. Jot down what God speaks to you in prayer and reflect on it daily.

DIRECTIONS:

1. Fill in the large circles first: What's right? What do I care about? What bothers me about the world?

2. Identify your moral values, convictions and passions by looking at the overlaps between the large circle categories.

3. Determine your Personal Moral Imperative by discovering how your values, convictions and passions overlap to create opportunities for action.

my personal moral imperative

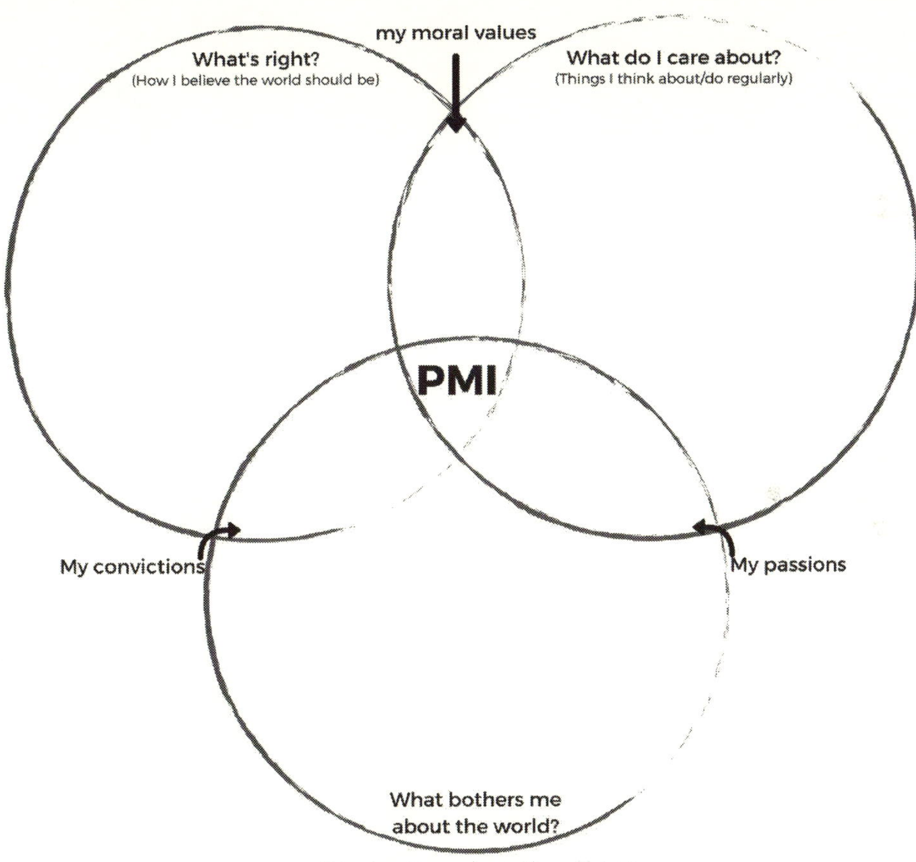

My Personal Moral Imperative

What am I passionate about changing in the world that I would spend everyday working on if I could?

notes

 "Your time is limited, so don't waste it living someone else's life." – Steve Jobs

notes

"Each of us has a personal calling... and that the best way to succeed is to discover what you love and then find a way to offer it to others..." – Oprah Winfrey

free space

"If you want to identify me... ask me what I am living for... ask me what I think is keeping me from living fully for the thing I want to live for." – Thomas Merton

free space

"The purpose of life is not to be happy. It is to...have it make some difference that you have lived and lived well." – Ralph Waldo Emerson

God's game plan

"For I know the plans I have for you," says the Lord. "They are plans for good and not for disaster, to give you a future and a hope." (Jeremiah 29:11, NLT)

In the back of our minds, we believe God must know what He's doing, and we (maybe sometimes with more difficulty than other times) hold Him to His promise to work everything together for our good (see Romans 8:28). The challenge comes when we don't understand His plan, His purpose, or how the struggle we're facing today could possibly be for our good when it looks like a disaster.

The truth is, the more we seek God and ask Him to reveal His purpose and plan for our lives, the clearer the big picture will become. He probably won't answer with a play-by-play account of what to do, where to go, and what's going to happen. However, He will come through on His promises to prosper us if we are committed to living according to His Word. In the times that we have to wait on God, we are building our faith and confidence in Him. Discovering God's plan for our lives is not just about figuring out what He has for us. It's about knowing Him as our Savior, our Heavenly Father, and our friend.

We must align our will and vision for our lives with God's by staying connected to Him. We do that by earnestly seeking Him and living in accordance with His Word. Even when it looks like the plan is failing and isn't going to work out, remember David's words:

"The Lord will work out his plans for my life—for your faithful love, O Lord, endures forever. Don't abandon me, for you made me." (Psalm 138:8, NLT)

Be encouraged! God does have a plan; it's the very reason He made you. And He will lead you if you stay close enough to hear His voice.

CONSIDER THIS:
Has God given you a glimpse of His plan for your life? Has He shown you where He's taking you?

TAKE ACTION:
Invite God to walk with you today. Talk to Him throughout the day, seeking His insight as you face decisions or challenges.

If we let Him, God will use all of who we are for the fulfillment of His purpose. In prayer, ask God to reveal His plans for activating His purpose through the areas of your life listed on the next page. Jot down what comes to you. Pray about how you can start taking steps toward putting His plan into action.

Godly insight on...

My gifts:

My habits:

My priorities:

My ministry:

My career:

My family:

My dreams:

My relationships:

notes

"Always go with your passions. Never ask yourself if it's realistic or not."
– Deepak Chopra

notes

"True happiness... is not attained through self-gratification, but through fidelity to a worthy purpose." – Helen Keller

free space

"There is a plan and a purpose, a value to every life, no matter what its location, age, gender or disability." – Sharron Angle

free space

"Definiteness of purpose is the starting point of all achievement."
– W. Clement Stone

dream

let your passion fuel your purpose

Lord Jesus, thank You for helping me understand my true mission and purpose. Reveal to me Your plans for my life and how I can activate the special gifts, passions and resources You've given me the way You intended. Show me the path I should take, and help me to keep my heart open to Your guidance.

...with faith

You can never please God without faith, without depending on him. Anyone who wants to come to God must believe that there is a God and that he rewards those who sincerely look for him. (Hebrews 11:6, TLB)

There comes a time when we find ourselves at a point of tension, or even grief, as we're faced with the contrast of what is and what we believe should be in the world. As God continues to reveal His plan for our lives, we get glimpses of how we'll be able to achieve our personal missions; but we'll still have to overcome obstacles along the way. It's in those times that we must be able to stand confidently on God's Word, claim His promises, and have faith that He will work everything out on our behalf as we strive to do His Will.

As you think about your Personal Purpose, consider the intricacies of your moral imperative: the problem you wish to solve and what it will take to achieve that ideal reality. Remember, God doesn't expect you to figure it all out or make it happen on your own! Faith is about believing in and depending on God both to help us do what we can and to go above and beyond our ability to do what we can't.

CONSIDER THIS:

Think back to when you first identified your passion(s) connected to your Personal Moral Imperative. How can your passions be applied to fulfilling your Personal Moral Imperative?

What, specifically, will you have to rely on faith for as you seek to connect your passions to your personal mission?

TAKE ACTION:

Work through the thought map on the next page to identify your Passion-Driven Dream. Your Passion-Driven Dream is the visualization of how your personal mission can be activated to make a difference in the world by responding to your Personal Moral Imperative. It's what the ideal world would look like as you use your gifts, experiences, and passions to positively impact others around you. Identifying your Passion-Driven Dream will help answer the "How do I live out my personal mission and purpose?" question.

my passion-driven dream

My moral values, convictions and passions are...

PMI

I must activate them to make a difference in...

My personal mission is to use...

These gifts:

These passions:

These strengths:

to...

create / start / build / do

(circle one)

What?

In order to change...

And make a difference by...

MY PASSION-DRIVEN DREAM

notes

"Build your own dreams, or someone else will hire you to build theirs."
– Dr. Farrah Gray

notes

"Your dream is the key to your future... You need a dream, if you're going to succeed in anything you do." – Mark Gorman

free space

free space

"Risk more than others think is safe. Care more than others think is wise. Dream more than others think is practical. Expect more than others think is possible."
– Cadet Maxim

...with compassion

Don't be concerned for your own good but for the good of others. (1 Corinthians 10:24, NLT)

Our compassion for others is what allows us to act on their behalf, even when it isn't convenient, easy, or to our own advantage. It is compassion that marked all of Jesus' miraculous works, and it is compassion that each of us needs in order to follow His example of serving others in love.

It's far too easy to allow our own schedules, preferences or mood hold us back from the ministry of compassionate service God has called us to. Everyday we need God's help to see past ourselves, to truly be in the moment and not miss opportunities to use what we've been given to make a difference in the lives of those who cross our paths.

Compassion isn't easy, but it is an integral part of our God-given mission and purpose. When placed at the center of our personal missions, it serves as an anchor that ties us to Jesus' method of effective, meaningful ministry. He was—and still is!—all about meeting people where they are and addressing their most pressing needs. We can't do that without compassion and a heart for serving others.

CONSIDER THIS:
How has compassion shaped your Passion-Driven Dream? What is it that stirs compassion within you and compels you to take action?

TAKE ACTION:
Part of casting a vision or launching a new idea—whether it be for a new venture or a new lifestyle— is getting the people that matter to identify with your mission. Using the description of your Passion-Driven Dream, write a mission statement that describes how compassion plays a role in the action you want to take and how others' compassion for your cause will empower you to succeed.

In your prayer time, ask God to continue to give you a heart of compassion and the courage to seize opportunities to show compassion to others as you work toward fulfilling your Passion-Driven Dream.

my compassion-driven mission

Mission Statement
Brief summary of my values and how I aim to carry them out.

I will show compassion by...
How will I integrate acts of compassion into the heart of what I do?

Others' compassion will fuel my mission by...
What and how can other people give to help me achieve my Passion-Driven Dream?

notes

"I think of myself as a catalyst of action and a messenger of hope, turning people onto themselves and turning people onto their dreams." – Les Brown

notes

free space

"No act of kindness, however small, is ever wasted." – Aesop

free space

...with generosity

Give away your life; you'll find life given back, but not merely given back—given back with bonus and blessing. Giving, not getting, is the way. Generosity begets generosity. (Luke 6:38, MSG)

We know "it is more blessed to give than to receive" (see Acts 20:35), but somehow it can seem much more easily said than done. With our own sets of responsibilities, struggles, goals and dreams to consider, it's a challenge to take care of ourselves and our families with the scarce time and resources we have each day. What can we possibly spare to give, and how?

King Solomon wisely observed that when we pour out, God promises to fill us up again: ***"The generous will prosper; those who refresh others will themselves be refreshed." (Proverbs 11:25, NLT)*** The more we give, the more He gives back. Even though sometimes it may seem like you don't have a single dollar, minute, or ounce of energy left to give, when you trust God and commit your actions to Him, He promises not only to honor your sacrifice but also to revitalize you in the process! The more we give, the more we receive. We become stronger, more vibrant individuals fueled by our outpouring of Christ's love to others.

"Generosity begets generosity." That's a powerful law of nature that holds true in both the physical and spiritual realms. We've heard it countless times: "You can't out-give God." Well, has that ever *not* been the case in your life? Remember, we are blessed to be a blessing. God gives to us so that we may give to others. We open up the channels to receive His blessings when we allow ourselves to be a conduit instead of a container. The outflow is essential; or else we end up like the Dead Sea—with no outflow, life cannot thrive. By generously pouring out of ourselves, we constantly make room for God to pour in more of what He has for us. As a result, there's a free flow of God's love and blessings through us to others.

CONSIDER THIS:

Compassion-driven acts of generosity have the potential to change lives and the world. Think about the child that is one meal away from starvation; the father that is one suit away from finally landing the job that will support his family; or the organization that is one grant away from having to close its doors to the people it serves. What impact could your generosity have?

TAKE ACTION:

On the next page, map out how generosity can fuel the achievement of your Passion-Driven Dream. Think about what it is you ultimately want to give others in order to fulfill your mission and Personal Moral Imperative. Consider how supporters of your vision might be willing to give their time, knowledge or resources to empower you to do so. Identify different ways you can inspire those you will reach to pay it forward.

Get in the flow! Give away one thing today that will help someone else in need.

live to give
me to others
GENEROSITY BEGETS GENEROSITY
Luke 6:38
others to me
others pay it forward

notes

"There are no traffic jams along the extra mile." – Roger Staubach

notes

 "Life isn't about getting and having, it's about giving and being." – Kevin Kruse

free space

"The willingness to share does not make one charitable; it makes one free."
– Robert Brault

free space

"We make a living by what we get, but we make a life by what we give."
– Winston Churchill

...with an open heart

Take delight in the Lord, and he will give you the desires of your heart. (Psalm 37:4, NIV)

Often times, that verse of Scripture is interpreted to mean that if we do the things God wants us to do, He'll give us whatever we desire to have. But is that what we really want? How many times have you devised the perfect strategy only for it to crumble right in front of you despite your best efforts? How many times have you said, "If I just have *(fill in the blank)*, everything will be fine"? How did that turn out?

In all your dreaming, stay open to the leading of the Lord. Once we finally lock into our passion and start envisioning the many ways to activate it, we can all too easily get backlogged in the "mental download" process. Our focus subtly shifts from diligently listening for God's voice of direction to the dozens of ideas and to-dos popping into our minds all at once now that we have a concept to run with. We have to stay anchored by the voice of God, always leaving Him at the helm.

Another way to understand that verse is this: If we seek after God and strive to please Him in our everyday lives, He will place in our hearts the desires *He wants us to have*—desires that reflect what He cares about most.

Have you ever heard anyone say something like, "The best plans you can make yourself will always fall short of what God has planned for you"? Well, it's true! What if we tapped into what God wanted for us—His plans for our lives—and started desiring those things? How much better would things turn out then? God knows more and thinks bigger than we ever could. If we let Him do the planning, we'll enjoy a life more abundant than we could ever imagine.

Solomon, in all his wisdom, left us this critical reminder:

Trust God from the bottom of your heart; don't try to figure out everything on your own. Listen for God's voice in everything you do, everywhere you go; he's the one who will keep you on track. (Proverbs 3:5–6, MSG)

If God saw fit to instill in you the passions, dreams and desires you have, why wouldn't He also show you how to activate them? In fact, Jesus is the best advisor we could ever have. He knows EVERYTHING! Past, present and future are all in His purview; and when the life we're striving for is the one He lived, that makes Him the single best leader to follow. Spending time daily connecting with Him through prayer and reading His Word will ensure that you receive the proper guidance on your journey to fulfilling your Passion-Driven Dream.

CONSIDER THIS:

It's easy to get carried away with the magnitude of your Personal Purpose or Passion-Driven Dream. When we get excited about a new idea or adventure, before we know it we've run off planning every detail that comes to mind without first stopping to consult God about the best course of action to take. Consider including Jesus in your planning process by trusting Him to put the right things in your heart and letting Him lead the way.

TAKE ACTION:
In your prayer time today, reserve a few minutes to listen for God's direction. Sometimes it helps to get up early before everyone else's day starts to minimize distractions. Clear your mind and just listen. When we give God the opportunity to speak to us, He does. Write down what He speaks to you about your dream and compare it with your own plans. Are there any changes that need to be made? Are there any priorities that need to be reorganized?

checking in with God

What I'm thinking:

God's insight:

Things to prioritize:

Goals to strive for:

Steps to get there:

notes

"Dream big dreams. Purpose in your heart that you're going to do something for God that nobody has ever done before." – Jack Cunningham

notes

"Dreaming, after all, is a form of planning." – Gloria Steinem

free space

"Certain things catch your eye, but pursue only those that capture the heart."
– Ancient Indian Proverb

free space

"The world changes according to the way people see it, and if you can alter, even by a millimeter, the way people look at reality, then you can change the world."
– James Baldwin

define

framing your vision

Lord Jesus, I trust Your plan for my life. Show me how to fit together the gifts and passions You've given me so that I may live out my mission and purpose in a way that generates meaningful impact.

your God-driven vision

This vision is for a future time. It describes the end, and it will be fulfilled. If it seems slow in coming, wait patiently, for it will surely take place. It will not be delayed. (Habakkuk 2:3, NLT)

English author and poet James Allen wrote, "Dream lofty dreams, and as you dream, so shall you become. Your Vision is the promise of what you shall one day be. Your Ideal is the prophecy of what you shall at last unveil."

A vision is born when a Passion-Driven Dream is operationalized through a strategic plan of action. It is the encapsulation of your God-given Personal Purpose in an actionable framework. As you start to build your dream's framework, it's important to keep God as the chief architect.

As we strive to harness our passion with purpose, it is our diligence and our resolve that transform our dreams into operable visions. And if it is your vision that defines what you ultimately become, you must take great care in crafting and maintaining it.

Vision is important. Without vision, we live aimlessly and can wind up self-destructing. The Bible says, *Where there is no vision, the people perish..." (Proverbs 29:18, KJV)* We need something to strive for; something that encompasses all we are, hope to be, and want to achieve in the world—not to mention, what God has called us to accomplish for His Kingdom.

God is sure to see our visions through to fruition as long as we remain faithful and in alignment with Him. So though the task may seem daunting, remember nothing's too hard for God (see Jeremiah 32:17). He promised to keep you on track, and He's sure to fulfill His Word; just keep following in faith!

CONSIDER THIS:

How can you turn your Passion-Driven Dream into an actionable vision? What would it look like? Does it begin with making changes in your daily lifestyle? Can you team up with others already serving a similar vision, or will you need to start something new?

TAKE ACTION:

As God told the prophet Habakkuk, *"Write the vision, and make it plain..." (Habakkuk 2:2, KJV)* Map out a framework for what your Passion-Driven Dream looks like in action. We'll call it your God-Driven Vision.

To build out your vision, describe how you'll use your gifts to serve others, showing them the love of Christ by addressing a real challenge in their lives. If you're considering launching a new endeavor to capture your vision, use these prompts as a guide:

- What essential resources will I need to begin? (E.g. time, money, space, skills or software, support of others, etc.)

- What will be the core activities involved in achieving my Passion-Driven Dream?

- What materials might I need to collect or create? Which programs will I need to adapt or design, and what products or services will I need to package and present?

· What are the outcomes I hope to achieve? (Think of outcomes as shorter-term results.)

· What is the long-term impact I desire to have? Vividly define it and keep this as your overall vision statement. Use your Personal Moral Imperative as a guide here. It might be helpful to look up different companies' or nonprofit organizations' vision statements to get a feel for this.

Read your vision statement daily! It will serve as an anchor to your faith, a source of inspiration, and a reminder of what you're striving to achieve.

Pray for greater clarity and discernment so that as you begin to do your part, you remain sharply in tune with God's vision for your life and continue to be led by Him.

my God-driven vision

Essential resources:

Core activities:

Critical materials:

Expected outcomes:
(Short-term results)

Anticipated impact:
(Long-term results)

My vision statement:
(A brief aspirational description of what I'm striving to accomplish)

notes

 "You are never too old to set another goal or to dream a new dream." – C. S. Lewis

notes

"The best way to succeed is to have a specific Intent, a clear Vision, a plan of Action, and the ability to maintain Clarity." – Steve Maraboli

free space

"Efforts and courage are not enough without purpose and direction."
– John F. Kennedy

free space

"If you set goals and go after them with all the determination you can muster, your gifts will take you places that will amaze you." – Les Brown

your scope

Do your planning and prepare your fields before building your house. (Proverbs 24:27, NLT)

You wouldn't trust an architect that built a house without blueprints, would you? In the same way, we must engage in a diligent planning process in order to get a clear picture of how we'll see our visions accomplished.

Due diligence begins with first scoping out the extent of the problem before announcing any plans of action. This is a critical step, as it's essential that you have a thorough understanding of the landscape you're entering before you get to work. You'll need to be intimately familiar with the history and context of the challenge you want to address and key factors that perpetuate the problem.

Defining your scope is like setting the rules of engagement. Once you have an understanding of the problem, you can narrowly identify the specific aspects of the problem you want to work on. Your scope must be specific and set clear parameters for what you'll do and why. This will help to make it easier to vet opportunities as they arise and determine if they fit with your mission and vision, or if they're beyond your reach.

Take a look at the landscape—the field in which your vision falls—and see what's out there that you can learn from and apply to your vision's framework. Doing so will help you understand what's currently being done or what's already been attempted, as well as identify peers and potential partners. Also take note of any programs or policies that are in place (or pending), as those can influence the way you take action, too. (This won't apply to every vision, but it may be relevant to those related to serving specific in-need communities or age groups).

While doing your research and drafting your plan, keep this proverb in mind: *"Any enterprise is built by wise planning, becomes strong through common sense, and profits wonderfully by keeping abreast of the facts." (Proverbs 24:3–4, TLB)*

It's important to stay in touch with technological advances, industry trends and best practices, and knowledge banks; or, if your vision is more personal in nature, you'll want to take note of any current or recent happenings that could affect your approach. These can be great resources for you, especially if your vision is to start a new business, awareness initiative, or charitable organization. However, be careful not to let these things alone define your scope. Always hold on to the purpose, passion and vision God has given you! But do use what's available to you for your advantage.

CONSIDER THIS:

It's said, "If your dreams don't scare you, they aren't big enough." Is the scope of your vision limited to things you believe you can accomplish in your own power, or will you have to rely on God's supernatural power to make your Passion-Driven Dream a reality? Listen to what God is speaking to your heart to do, and embrace it in faith. If it seems impossible, that means He's signing up to do what you can't.

TAKE ACTION:

Do your research! Spend some time investigating the landscape and defining how your vision can generate or amplify impact in your specific problem area. Map out the specific resources, processes, support systems and other core elements that you'll need to put in place in order for your vision to come to life. Keep these things in prayer and have faith that God will empower you to make your Passion-Driven Dream a reality!

Draft your Action Plan. This ties together all the elements you've worked on thus far (your Personal Moral Imperative, your Compassion-Driven Mission and your God-Driven Vision) along with key elements from your scoping research to create one big picture to keep you moving forward. Use the Mad Lib-style template included in the next few pages to get started.

Vision Scoping

Research notes:

Purpose peers:
(Those serving a similar mission)

Points of differentiation:
(What makes my approach unique)

Points of alignment:
(Synergies that exist between me and my purpose peers)

Required resources:

Key contacts:

Critical infrastructure:

vision action planning mad-lib

I want to use my passion for ___________________________
(something I'm passionate about)

to change the world by ___________________________ .
(how I'll do it)

I'll use my skills in _____________ and _____________
(talent/skill)   (talent/skill)

to ___________________________ .
(action)

This will require support from ___________________________ ,
(person/business/organization)

___________________________ , and ___________________________ .
(person/business/organization)   (person/business/organization)

To get started, I need ___________________________ ,
(resource)

___________________________ , and ___________________________ .
(resource)   (resource)

Key starter steps include ___________________________ ,
(step 1)

___________________________ , and ___________________________ .
(step 2)   (step 3)

supporting scriptures

additional resources

notes

"Nothing is impossible, the word itself says, 'I'm possible!'" – Audrey Hepburn

notes

"First, have a definite, clear practical ideal; a goal, an objective. Second, have the necessary means to achieve your ends; wisdom, money, materials, and methods. Third, adjust all your means to that end." – Aristotle

free space

"If you aren't diligently working towards changing something that bothers you, you rescind your right to complain about it." – Rob Liano

free space

"Start by doing what's necessary; then do what's possible; and suddenly you are doing the impossible." – St. Francis of Assisi

with diligence

Lord Jesus, thank You for opening my mind and heart to perceive the vision You have for my life. Help me to continually seek You first as I strive to live out Your perfect plan. Give me the grace to be diligent and disciplined and put action behind my faith in my journey to fulfill the mission and purpose You've crafted for me.

activate your faith

So you see, it isn't enough just to have faith. You must also do good to prove that you have it. Faith that doesn't show itself by good works is no faith at all— it is dead and useless. (James 2:17, TLB)

It's one thing to say you have faith. It's another thing entirely to act on it. Actions not only speak louder than words, they get more things done, too. We must operationalize our faith by doing the things that will result in success. As God gives clarity and direction and opens doors, we must move forward, continually doing our part to bring the vision to life.

You're right, there's no way you can make it all happen on your own; and God isn't asking you to! He's asking you to move forward as He leads and to trust Him to do what you can't. Every great vision becomes a reality one step at a time; but you must initiate the process in order to get results! You can't say you're an inventor if you don't create something new. You're not an entrepreneur until you pull the trigger and go into business for yourself. You'll always be the same person you are if you don't actively work on changing the things you wish to improve. You have to *do something.* The results will speak for themselves.

James recounts the story of Abraham to teach us a valuable lesson about the need for both faith and action:

Don't you remember that our ancestor Abraham was shown to be right with God by his actions when he offered his son Isaac on the altar? You see, his faith and his actions worked together. His actions made his faith complete. (James 2:21–22, NLT)

Faith alone does not bring our dreams, goals and visions to life. It takes action.

CONSIDER THIS:
What's standing in the way of you putting your faith into action? What are you worried about, afraid or unsure of?

TAKE ACTION:
A Faith Manifesto is a personal statement of faith-fueled empowerment that dispels fears, doubts and insecurities one by one with the declarations and promises found in God's Word. Take some time today to get into your Bible and create your own Faith Manifesto using the example on the next page as a guide. Think about all the things that are holding you back from activating your faith, and turn them around by comparing each one with a verse that affirms what God has to say about you and about your vision.

Put your Faith Manifesto somewhere you can see it (maybe on your mirror, refrigerator or bedroom door) and read it daily along with your mission and vision statements as a personal source of encouragement and confidence.

my faith manifesto

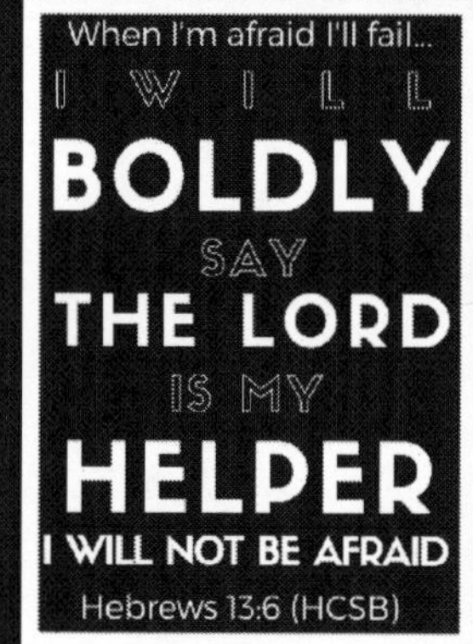

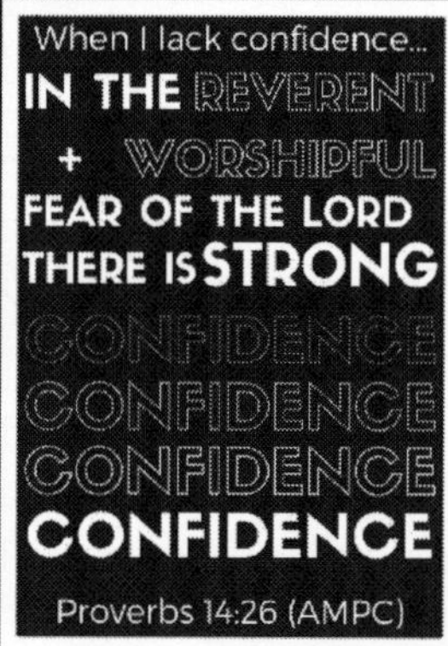

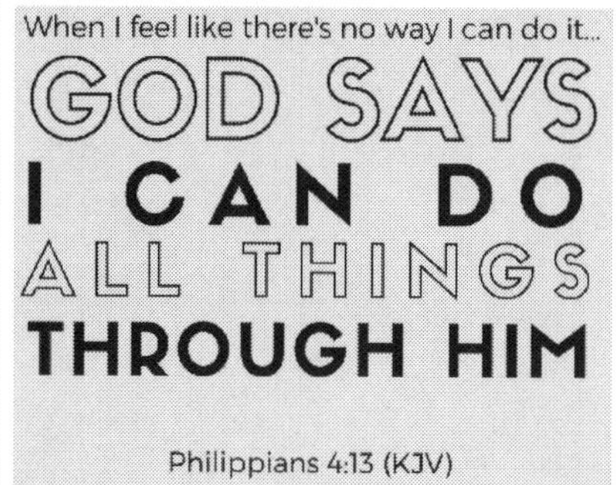

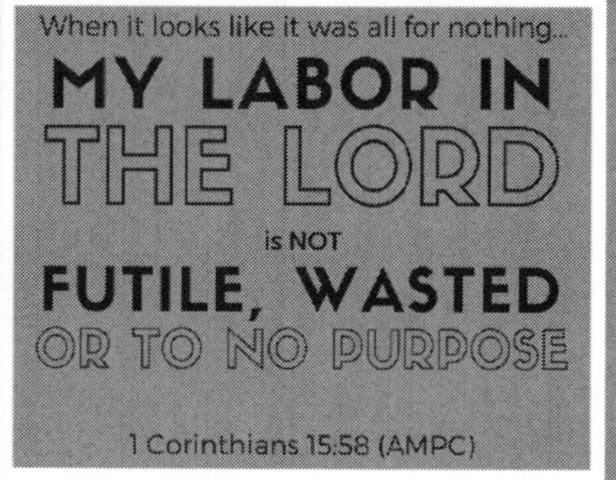

When I don't think I have what it takes...
I AM FEARFULLY & WONDERFULLY MADE
Psalm 139:14 (KJV)
When I'm not sure which way to go...
HE WILL SHOW ME WHICH PATH TO TAKE
Proverbs 3:6 (NLT)
When I'm afraid I'll fail...
I WILL BOLDLY SAY THE LORD IS MY HELPER
I WILL NOT BE AFRAID
Hebrews 13:6 (HCSB)
When I lack confidence...
IN THE REVERENT + WORSHIPFUL FEAR OF THE LORD THERE IS STRONG
CONFIDENCE
CONFIDENCE
CONFIDENCE
CONFIDENCE
Proverbs 14:26 (AMPC)
When nothing makes sense...
I WILL LEAN ON + TRUST IN + BE CONFIDENT IN THE LORD
Proverbs 3:5 (AMPC)
When I feel like there's no way I can do it...
GOD SAYS I CAN DO ALL THINGS THROUGH HIM
Philippians 4:13 (KJV)
When it looks like it was all for nothing...
MY LABOR IN THE LORD is NOT FUTILE, WASTED OR TO NO PURPOSE
1 Corinthians 15:58 (AMPC)

notes

"The only people who never tumble are those who never mount the high wire."
– Oprah Winfrey

notes

"When I dare to be powerful, to use my strength in the service of my vision, then it becomes less and less important whether I am afraid." – Audre Lorde

free space

free space

 "Four things for success: work and pray, think and believe." – Norman Peale

start now

Farmers who wait for perfect weather never plant. If they watch every cloud, they never harvest. (Ecclesiastes 11:4, NLT)

Have you ever decided to start a diet or new workout routine, or even break a bad habit, and told yourself, "I'll start on Monday"? What happened when Monday came? The best thing to do is start right now when you're motivated and buzzing with ideas.

Don't put off getting started until everything is perfect and you have everything you think you need. Guess what? That day will never come. There will always be *just one more thing* that needs to happen. Life is notorious for letting little things pop up to derail our best-laid plans. Don't let your dream be deferred. Tomorrow isn't promised!

Proverbs 13:12 says, ***"Hope deferred makes the heart sick, but a dream fulfilled is a tree of life." (NLT)*** Start today and get on your way to seeing your God-Driven Vision fulfilled!

CONSIDER THIS:

What actions can you take to begin bringing your vision to fulfillment? Do you need to do some more research? Follow up with a potential teammate? Put in a call to someone who could open a door for you?

TAKE ACTION:

On the next page, make a Daily Diligence Checklist of 5 things you can do every day to further your God-Driven Vision... and get it done! Whether it's researching the latest developments in your field, reaching out to people you'd like to mentor you or partner with you, writing up your idea to develop an actionable and presentable plan... there are countless things you can do that will incrementally build your momentum.

daily diligence checklist

✔ **Reflect**

✔ **Research**

✔ **Reach out**

✔ **Revise**

✔ **Realize**

notes

"To accomplish great things we must first dream, then visualize, then plan... believe...act!" – Alfred Montapert

notes

free space

"How wonderful it is that nobody need wait a single moment before starting to improve the world." – Anne Frank

free space

"I have been impressed with the urgency of doing. Knowing is not enough; we must apply. Being willing is not enough; we must do." – Leonardo da Vinci

pick your team

Where there is no [wise, intelligent] guidance, the people fall [and go off course like a ship without a helm], But in the abundance of [wise and godly] counselors there is victory. (Proverbs 11:14, AMP)

Executing your vision will take great commitment, strong work ethic, and support from family, friends, community members and teammates that will take up your cause with you. Surround yourself with people who understand and identify with your Personal Purpose and vision who also have relevant experience that can catalyze your action plan.

It can be extremely life giving to receive support for your humble vision, especially when people believe in you enough to jump in and help. In order to fully leverage the support of others and effectively mobilize them, you need a very specific understanding of what needs to be accomplished and how others can help you.

It's important that you take the time to determine what exactly needs to be done and which particular qualities, experiences and skillsets are required to best complete the job. Be very diligent in creating a system that gets the right people involved in the right ways so that you can make the most of the passions, gifts and resources they're offering. When you pick your team, be sure those you choose to work with are given clear direction and that they come equipped to do their job. Whether you're picking a team to form an advisory board or a prayer circle, having people you can trust in your corner is vital!

CONSIDER THIS:
Who will you need on your team to bring your vision to life? Be prayerful in selecting others to be in your inner circle of supporters or share in the work. Ask God to lead you to the right partners, even if they're just partners in prayer or accountability.

TAKE ACTION:
After you've done your research and constructed the framework for your vision, connect with people in your network who can help get the ball rolling. Prayerfully fill in the roles on the next page to determine the key support functions you need, the responsibilities you envision the person in each role taking on, and the skills they should have to help propel your vision forward.

picking my team

Role: ____

Responsibilities:

Required skills:

Role: ____

Responsibilities:

Required skills:

Role: ____

Responsibilities:

Required skills:

notes

"When you're surrounded by people who share a passionate commitment around a common purpose, anything is possible." – Howard Schultz

notes

"Choose your friends with caution; plan your future with purpose, and frame your life with faith." – Thomas S. Monson

free space

free space

"A vision we give to others of who and what they could become has power when it echoes what the spirit has already spoken into their souls." – Larry Crabbe

be patient

So do not throw away this confident trust in the Lord. Remember the great reward it brings you! Patient endurance is what you need now, so that you will continue to do God's will. Then you will receive all that he has promised. (Hebrews 10:35–36, NLT)

It seems the way of life is that nothing goes smoothly forever. We're bound to encounter delays, obstacles, and detours as we endeavor to achieve our goals. These things are all tests of faith designed to make us stronger and more resilient and to increase our dependence on God.

As the Lord leads us through the unforeseen hills and turns, we learn to trust Him more and build the patience and endurance we need to see our vision to fulfillment. *"For you know that when your faith is tested, your endurance has a chance to grow." (James 1:3, NLT)*

Sometimes, despite our best efforts to diligently do our part, things don't seem to fall into place or gain momentum as we'd hoped or anticipated. It can feel like there's something we must have missed or something we're not doing quite right, and we rack our brains trying to figure it out. Or worse, we end up overexerting ourselves trying to do more and more in our own strength to make everything work. And when it doesn't, it can feel like it's all for nothing. But that's not the case! Paul's reminder to the Corinthian believers is still applicable to us today: *"Therefore, my dear brothers, be steadfast, immovable, always excelling in the Lord's work, knowing that your labor in the Lord is not in vain."* *(1 Corinthians 15:58, HCSB)*

We must stand firm and be patient, waiting for God to act on our behalf. He gave us a vision and a promise, and because of who He is, His Word will always hold true. So as you continue to piece together your action plan, and even as you begin to carry it out, if things just don't seem to be coming together, don't give up. Keep doing your part—and only *your* part—diligently, and trust God for the rest. Remember, His plans are often different from ours, but they always exceed our expectations when they come to fruition.

"So let's not get tired of doing what is good. At just the right time we will reap a harvest of blessing if we don't give up." *(Galatians 6:9, NLT)*

CONSIDER THIS:

Think back on the various things God has told you and showed you about your life over the years. Which of those things have already happened? With regard to your vision action plan, what can you already see fitting together?

TAKE ACTION:

In moments when you're waiting for God to take action on your behalf, it's good to remind yourself of His promises. If you've already encountered a challenge, whether it is a mental roadblock or another barrier to progress, take a moment to revisit or even add to your Faith Manifesto. Think about the promises written in His Word and compare them to the obstacle you're currently facing. Could it be that God is still working, but in a different way than you expected? Feel free to write in the notes pages as you reflect.

Keep up with your Daily Diligence Checklist and trust God to do what you can't!

notes

"We should not look back unless it is to derive useful lessons from past errors, and for the purpose of profiting by dearly bought experience." – George Washington

notes

"I'm reflective only in the sense that I learn to move forward.
I reflect with a purpose." – Kobe Bryant

free space

"People often say that motivation doesn't last. Well, neither does bathing. That's why we recommend it daily." – Zig Ziglar

free space

come what may

Not that I was ever in need, for I have learned how to be content with whatever I have. I know how to live on almost nothing or with everything. I have learned the secret of living in every situation, whether it is with a full stomach or empty, with plenty or little. For I can do everything through Christ, who gives me strength. (Philippians 4:11–13, NLT)

Every endeavor encounters obstacles along the way; as the vision caster, it is your job to keep your team encouraged and be diligent in reevaluating and revising the plan as needs arise.

On Paul's mission to share the gospel, he encountered every setback imaginable. From shipwrecks to imprisonment to torture, he surmounted every obstacle by God's grace. Learning to be content in every situation and recognizing it was by God's strength alone that he could achieve anything at all empowered Paul to confidently move forward in the face of opposition. In the same way, our ability to seek God, adapt to circumstances that arise, and revise our game plan accordingly will keep us functioning within our Personal Purpose and will help us see our God-Driven Vision through to completion.

Acclaimed poet Maya Angelou described the ideal mindset when it comes to pressing toward any goal: "Hoping for the best, prepared for the worst, and unsurprised by anything in between." As a visionary, you have the unique challenge of optimistically staying focused on the end goal while acknowledging the setbacks and obstacles that emerge along the way. Don't let opposition derail you. Instead, plan to overcome it.

Preparation is essential and faith even more so. Recognize bumps in the road are inevitable, and when you reach one, remember God's promises and encourage your team to hold on to their faith. Be flexible and adapt your approach to account for the challenge in front of you, and lead your team through the valley with transparency, patience, and hope. Stay open to ideas and feedback from partners and trusted advisors, but never let go of the vision God outlined for you. Carry out the plan in a way that both propels you toward the end goal and manages the situation in front of you. Learn to be content in whatever situation you're facing, like Paul did, realizing it's just part of the journey. God has an expected end in mind for you; so don't worry. Remember Jeremiah 29:11.

CONSIDER THIS:

What's your natural reaction to opposition? Do you instantly get worried and run through countless if-then scenarios? Does giving up cross your mind? Do you jump into Plan B without a second thought?

TAKE ACTION:

The Psalmist penned the following prayer: *"Lead me in the right path, O Lord, or my enemies will conquer me. Make your way plain for me to follow." (Psalm 5:8, NLT)* While we may not have foes hunting us down like David did, fear and doubt can be some of the most formidable enemies we face. Ask God for fresh inspiration to re-envision a challenge you're facing as a new opportunity.

On the next page, examine a particular problem you've come

against in implementing your vision. What specific challenges does that problem create? How does it prevent you from fulfilling your mission? Next, jot down the current methods you're using to tackle the problem and think about some alternate ways you could work around it. Seek out fresh ideas and new insights from people you trust, experts in your field and others working toward a similar mission (your "purpose peers").

Prayerfully begin to put your new plan into action. As you move forward, keep track of what you learn works and what doesn't— through both research and experience— so you can refer to those insights as your vision continues to take shape.

contingency planning

The problem:

Challenges posed:

My current approach:

Alternate approach:

Purpose peers:

Their approach:

Takeaways & new inspiration:

notes

"A goal is not always meant to be reached, it often serves simply as something to aim at." – Bruce Lee

notes

"If you don't love what you're doing with unbridled passion and enthusiasm, you're not going to succeed when you hit obstacles." – Howard Schultz

free space

"The person who says it cannot be done should not interrupt the person who is doing it." – Chinese Proverb

free space

"If God puts a dream in your spirit...there is no power on this earth and there's no devil in hell that can stop that dream from coming to pass." – Jack Cunningham

act in love

Mostly what God does is love you. Keep company with him and learn a life of love. Observe how Christ loved us. His love was not cautious but extravagant. He didn't love in order to get something from us but to give everything of himself to us. Love like that. (Ephesians 5:2, MSG)

At the start of this journey we discovered that, as Christians, our lives are to reflect the example of Christ—one defined by the ultimate expression of love and selflessness. The passions grafted into your heart, the gifts you were given, and the sphere of influence you operate in were all intricately fit together for you to uniquely express God's love to others.

The way we reflect Christ is through the way we activate our passions, gifts and influence to show love to those around us. The way we love is what identifies us as Christians. As John 13:35 says, *"Your love for one another will prove to the world that you are my disciples." (NLT)*

Jesus gave His life as the ultimate expression of love and did so for the sole purpose of restoring His creation to the perfect state that would allow us to spend eternity with Him. As we persevere in our commitment to living a life that uses what we've been uniquely gifted to demonstrate the love of Christ to others, we will succeed in pointing them toward the One who loves them most. As you go through your day, remember the purpose driving your good deeds. The Apostle Paul put it this way: *"If I gave everything I have to the poor and even sacrificed my body, I could boast about it; but if I didn't love others, I would have gained nothing."* (1 Corinthians 13:3, NLT)

CONSIDER THIS:
It's so easy to get bogged down in the to-dos that we lose touch with the purpose driving our visions. Don't forget, love is both the means and the end. Remember to be diligent in reflecting God's love in your every action as you strive to fulfill your vision.

TAKE ACTION:
Not only are we to let love lead our actions, but we should encourage those around us to do the same. Hebrews 10:24 says, *"Let us think of ways to motivate one another to acts of love and good works." (NLT)* Think about how your vision can inspire or empower others to make a difference in their own way. Work through the thought map on the next page to supplement your mission and vision with activities specifically designed to spur others to positive action.

empower others through love

Mentor:

Someone I love:

Someone in need:

Someone with a dream:

Give:

My time:

My expertise:

My resources:

BE A catalyst

Teach:

A skill:

A lesson learned:

A better way:

Create an opportunity:

For a friend:

For a colleague:

For a stranger:

notes

"Everybody can be great, because everybody can serve. You only need a heart full of grace, a soul generated by love." – Dr. Martin Luther King, Jr.

notes

"We can't deliver folks from their pits, but we can sure get in there with them until God does." – Jen Hatmaker

free space

free space

"I expect to pass through this world but once. Any good work, therefore, any kind-ness, or any service I can render to any soul of man... let me do it now. Let me not neglect or defer it, for I shall not pass this way again." – Old Quaker Saying

be accountable

But I, the Lord, search all hearts and examine secret motives. I give all people their due rewards, according to what their actions deserve. (Jeremiah 17:10, NLT)

Making sure we're doing the right things is just part of the challenge to living out our personal mission and purpose from God. We must also ensure we're doing them for the right reasons. What God has called us to do is ultimately for His glory alone and so that the people around us can come to know Him for themselves through our expressions of His love.

How and why we do what we do is just as, if not more, important than what it is we're doing. 1 Samuel 13:14 reminds us, *"… the Lord has sought out a man after his own heart." (NLT)* It's what's in our hearts—our attitudes, intentions, and motives—that makes the difference. We can do all the right things, but if our hearts are not in the right place, it's meaningless (see Matthew 6:1-4).

As you implement the action plan you've prayerfully and diligently designed, consider how you will use your platform. Will your brand, program or personal character let God's love shine through and point people to Him? What drives you to utilize your gifts? Is it for wealth and fame, accolades and recognition, or something more eternal?

Ultimately, we are accountable to God for how we use what He's given us. Why not make the most of it?

CONSIDER THIS:

What drives you? Do your motives line up with the mission and purpose God designed for you?

TAKE ACTION:

On the next page, write down three core values you can use to evaluate any actions or decisions you make as you implement your action plan. Use this list as a filtering system that keeps you accountable to God's mission and purpose for your life as you pursue your God-Driven Vision.

decision diagnostic test

✔ Criterion #1
Stuck? Try to think of something that promotes consistency.

✔ Criterion #2
Stuck? Try to think of something that generates authenticity.

✔ Criterion #3
Stuck? Try to think of something that propels you toward where you want to go.

notes

"The right thing to do and the hard thing to do are usually the same."
– Steve Maraboli

notes

---

free space

"Follow the three R's: Respect for self. Respect for others. Responsibility for all your actions." – H. Jackson Brown, Jr.

free space

"It is not only what we do, but also what we do not do, for which we are accountable." –Molière

be rewarded

Whatever you do, work at it with all your heart, as though you were working for the Lord and not for people. Remember that the Lord will give you as a reward what he has kept for his people. For Christ is the real Master you serve. (Colossians 3:23-24, GNT)

You're the steward of the time you have. How you spend each hour and each day reflects your priorities and your Personal Purpose for your life. It takes great faith to choose to fill your time with things that reflect the vision and purpose God uniquely designed for you; but when you do, you'll find unparalleled peace and fulfillment.

God has a reward greater than we could ever imagine in store for us in Heaven. But He also pours out blessings and benefits to us here on Earth each day as we strive to please Him and do His Will. Take some time to read Psalm 112 – it's full of God's promises for abundant blessings we will enjoy as we strive to obey Him and follow the path He's laid out for us! God wants to give you abundant life: a life of health, joy, purpose and prosperity because He loves you and He chose you for Himself. But you have to choose Him, too.

Each day you wake up, you must choose either to go your own way or to let God fulfill His plans for your life. Choosing Christ isn't always the easiest path to take, but it's always worth it.

CONSIDER THIS:
What is your heart saying? Are you torn between the plans you've made and the path God is calling you to? Do you trust God to see His plans through and to take care of you every step of the way?

TAKE ACTION:
Pray about everything that's on your heart right now regarding the next step you feel led to take. Tell God everything you're unsure, worried, or fearful about, and ask Him for clarity, direction and reassurance. Make a commitment to pray daily and connect with God about your action plan before you start each day. Then, take Him with you. Include God in every decision, from the smallest to the biggest, and let Him lead you. You'll be amazed at how He responds and puts all the pieces together when you diligently seek Him!

prayer list

Direction:

Clarity:

Open doors:

Mentors:

Partners:

Victories:

Anxieties:

Obstacles:

notes

"When I stand before God at the end of my life, I would hope that I would not have
a single bit of talent left and could say, I used everything you gave me."
– Erma Bombeck

notes

"In the world, success is measured in terms of legacy, what we leave behind. In God's kingdom, success is measured by what we send on ahead." – Ron Brackin

free space

free space

"The reward of a work is to have produced it; the reward of effort is to have grown by it." – Antonin Sertillanges

wrap-up: a legacy of love

Your life is your legacy! What you choose to do with each day defines the impact you will have on others. Instead of waiting until you are near the end of your life, you can create your legacy here and now. Start living the way you want people to remember you. Do those things in your power that can help make the world the place you believe it should be—the way God intended it to be. Make your world a more loving, generous, forgiving, thoughtful, encouraging place. Lend a helping hand. Give someone a second chance. Bless a person in need. Build up a young person, teaching them what you wish someone had taught you. Show everyone you interact with the love of Christ.

In doing these things more and more, you'll build a legacy that lives and speaks for itself—and Christ—each day of your life and leaves a lasting impact on others for years to come.

What are you waiting for? Get started! You never know, you may be the only reflection of God someone will ever get the chance to see.

notes

"Leap and the net will appear." – Zen saying

notes

notes

"There's more at stake from the ripples we make than simply passing through."
– John Tracy Wilson

notes

"The choices we make about the lives we live determine the kinds of legacies we leave." – Tavis Smiley

notes

"Make someone feel something and you will never be forgotten."
– Charlotte Eriksson

notes

"In planning anything, the best place to begin is at the end. What outcome do you
want? How do you want to be remembered when you are gone?"
– Michael Hyatt

notes

"Some people wish it would happen, some people want it to happen, others make it happen." – Michael Jordan

notes

"Innovation is the art of creating a better, a more convenient and more comfortable way for the world to pass. Leaders leave footprints everywhere they go. They are impact makers and innovators." – Israelmore Ayivore

notes

"The souls of men are not measured by what they have done, but by what they leave behind." – Anonymous

notes

"Leave your legacy—not in possessions or accolades— but in moments. Moments that matter." – Alicia M. Smith

free space

 "You can't make a difference until you dare to be different." – Orrin Woodward

free space

"Those who bring excitement and enthusiasm to the lives of others won't be forgotten. Our legacy can be our positive attitude." – Farshad Asl

free space

"Strive not to be a success, but rather to be of value." – Albert Einstein

free space

"Few things are impossible to diligence and skill. Great works are performed not by strength, but by perseverance." – Samuel Johnson

free space

"Gardens are not made by singing 'Oh, how beautiful!' and sitting in the shade."
– Rudyard Kipling

free space

"Ordinary people who faithfully, diligently, and consistently do simple things that are right before God will bring forth extraordinary results."
– David A. Bednar

free space

"Whatever you can do, or dream you can, begin it. Boldness has genius, power and magic in it." – Johann Wolfgang von Goethe

free space

"Either you run the day, or the day runs you." – Jim Rohn

free space

"When we are gone, the only essential thing we will leave behind are the memories we create in the lives of those we have touched and those we love."
– Michael Hyatt

free space

"It's about the journey—mine and yours—and the lives we can touch, the legacy we can leave, and the world we can change for the better."
– Tony Dungy

about the author

Kendall Nelson is an author, impact strategy consultant and coach, and the steward of *Purposed to Impact*, a platform designed to equip and empower women to take their dreams of living in their God-given purpose from aspirational to attainable.

A self-proclaimed *Impact Catalyst*™, Kendall works with organizations and individuals alike to design and evaluate impact-driven action plans for their businesses, charitable initiatives and personal endeavors. As a coach, Kendall inspires and empowers her clients, helping them pinpoint their purpose and make a meaningful and measurable difference in the world.

Kendall is a wife, mommy, avid sports fan, professional multi-tasker, world traveler and nap enthusiast. She lives in Frederick, MD with her husband, Anthony, and their son, Jeremiah.

connect with Kendall

Real life:
Blog: www.lifepurposefull.com
Facebook: fb.com/lifepurposefull
Instagram: @lifepurposefull
Twitter: @lifepurposefull

Work life:
Book me: www.theimpactcatalyst.com
Facebook: fb.com/theimpactcatalyst
Instagram: @theimpactcatalyst
Twitter: @1impactcatalyst

about Purposed to Impact

Purposed to Impact is a platform curated to equip and empower men and women of faith to take their dreams of living in their God-given purpose from aspirational to attainable. Whether in print, online or in person, *Purposed to Impact* will help you pinpoint your God-given purpose and build it into an actionable strategy that finally allows you to do something meaningful and make a real difference in your world.

join the movement

Learn more: www.purposedtoimpact.com
Facebook Community: fb.com/purposedtoimpact

Made in the USA
Monee, IL
26 May 2020